perfect •
pizza

Published by:
TRIDENT REFERENCE PUBLISHING
801 12th Avenue South, Suite 400
Naples, Fl 34102 USA

Tel: + 1 (239) 649-7077
www.tridentreference.com
email: sales@tridentreference.com

perfect •
pizza

Perfect Pizza
© TRIDENT REFERENCE PUBLISHING

Publisher
Simon St. John Bailey

Editor-in-chief
Susan Knightley

Prepress
Precision Prep & Press

Includes Index
ISBN 1582797315
UPC 6 15269 97315 8

Printed in The United States

introduction

Keep your doors and windows shut when you cook
pizza or you may be bowled over in the
neighbourhood rush! The aroma is sensational!
Pizzas are easy and very satisfying to make
at home. There is no secret to success:
a well-kneaded dough and a tempting topping
of complementary ingredients are all it takes.

Apart from experimenting with a variety of flavors, try different shapes as well. The technique for homemade dough is extremely simple. Just dissolve yeast and sugar in warm water, set aside in a draught-free place until foamy. Stir in oil, sifted plain flour and salt and mix until a rough dough forms. Turn out onto a lightly floured surface and knead until soft and satiny, then let dough rise until it doubles its volume. Knock down and knead briefly before rolling out. For a thick crust, allow dough to rise again in pan.

Basic pizza dough can be prepared several days ahead and set aside to rise before being knocked down, covered with plastic food wrap and refrigerated. Bring to room temperature 2-3 hours before shaping and second rising, if desired.

Getting to Know Yeast

Yeast works best in warm conditions. Cold and draughts slow down its growth, whereas an intense heat will kill it.

Yeast works best when mixed with liquid that is at about 25°C/78°F. An easy way of making sure that the liquid is at the right temperature is to bring one-third of it to the boil and add the rest cold.

Using less yeast than required will cause the dough not to rise enough. Using too much yeast will give a crumbly, sour-tasting pizza base.

Dried yeast works as well as fresh but takes longer to activate and it is twice as concentrated as fresh yeast. Dried yeast will keep in a cool dark place for about six months. It will deteriorate if exposed to air.

Topping Cheeses

As Italy is the homeland of pizza, it is not surprising that cheese counts among favorite pizza toppings. The list of Italy's splendid cheeses is virtually endless, and even though mozzarella is the traditional pizza cheese, Parmesan, Gorgonzola, Provolone and ricotta are also frequently used to add special flavors.

Difficulty scale

■☐☐ I Easy to do

■■☐ I Requires attention

■■■ I Requires experience

basic
pizza dough

■□□ | Cooking time: 0 minute - Preparation time: 10 minutes

ingredients

> **1 teaspoon active dry yeast**
> **pinch sugar**
> **2/3 cup/170 ml/5 1/2 fl oz warm water**
> **2 cups/250 g/8 oz flour**
> **1/2 teaspoon salt**
> **1/4 cup/60 ml/2 fl oz olive oil**

tip from the chef

Try these tempting variations.
Herb pizza dough: Add 1 teaspoon dried mixed herbs to the flour mixture.
Cheese pizza dough: Add 60 g/2 oz grated tasty cheese (mature Cheddar) to the flour mixture.
Tomato pizza dough: Replace the water with 2/3 cup/170 ml/ 5 1/2 fl oz warmed tomato juice.
Wholemeal pizza dough: Replace half the flour with wholemeal flour. You may need to add a little extra water.

method

1. Place yeast, sugar and water in a large bowl and mix to dissolve. Set aside in a warm, draught-free place for 5 minutes or until foamy.

2. Place flour and salt in a food processor and pulse once or twice to sift. With machine running, slowly pour in oil and yeast mixture (a) and process to form a rough dough. Turn dough onto a lightly floured surface (b) and knead for 5 minutes or until soft and shiny. Add more flour if necessary.

3. Lightly oil a large bowl, then roll dough around in it to cover the surface with oil. Cover bowl tightly with plastic food wrap (c) and place in a warm, draught-free place for 1 1/2-2 hours or until dough has doubled in volume. Knock down (d) and remove dough from bowl. Knead briefly before using as desired.

....
Makes 250 g/8 oz dough

a

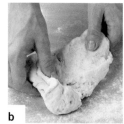
b

c

d

crispy wholemeal pizza

■□□ | Cooking time: 25 minutes - Preparation time: 10 minutes

method

1. Roll out dough to fit a 30 cm/12 in round pizza tray.
2. Heat oil in a frying pan, add onions and garlic, stir-fry until tender. Add tomatoes, basil and chilies. Simmer, uncovered, until reduced and thickened. Spread over dough base.
3. Arrange green pepper, pineapple and olives on top, sprinkle with mozzarella.
4. Bake in moderately hot oven for about 20 minutes or until crispy and golden brown.

....

Serves 6

ingredients

> 1 quantity wholemeal pizza dough (page 6)
> 2 tablespoons oil
> 2 onions, chopped
> 2 cloves garlic, crushed
> 425 g/13 1/2 oz canned tomatoes, undrained, crushed
> 1 tablespoon chopped fresh basil
> 2 small red chilies, chopped
> 1 green pepper, sliced
> 340 g/11 oz canned pineapple pieces, drained
> 6 stuffed olives, sliced
> 250 g/1/2 lb mozzarella cheese, grated

tip from the chef

Pizza makes a healthy meal, especially when made with a wholemeal base and served with a tossed green salad.

original
tomato pizzas

■□□ | Cooking time: 20 minutes - Preparation time: 10 minutes

method

1. Divide dough into 2 portions and shape each to form a 30 cm/12 in round. Place rounds on lightly greased baking trays and brush with oil.
2. Arrange half the tomato slices, garlic and oregano on top of each pizza base and season to taste with black pepper.
3. Bake at 200°C/400°F/Gas 6 for 15-20 minutes or until base is crisp and golden.

ingredients

> **2 quantities basic pizza dough (page 6)**
> **olive oil**
> **5 ripe tomatoes, sliced**
> **4 cloves garlic, sliced**
> **4 tablespoons fresh oregano leaves**
> **freshly ground black pepper**

....
Serves 8

tip from the chef

The simplest pizza of all, this one is best made with fresh young garlic. Any fresh herbs can be used in place of the oregano –marjoram, thyme and basil are all delicious alternatives.

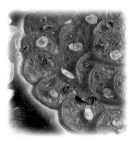

easy chili bean pizza

■□□ | Cooking time: 20 minutes - Preparation time: 5 minutes

ingredients

> 1 x 25 cm/10 in pizza base, homemade or purchased
> 440 g/14 oz canned chili beans
> 2 jalapeño chilies, seeded and sliced
> 250 g/8 oz mozzarella cheese, grated
> freshly ground black pepper
> 30 g/1 oz corn chips
> 3 tablespoons sour cream

method

1. Place pizza base on a lightly greased baking tray and top with beans. Sprinkle with chilies, mozzarella cheese and black pepper to taste.
2. Bake at 220°C/425°F/Gas 7 for 15-20 minutes or until base is crisp and golden.
3. To serve, top pizza with corn chips and sour cream.

....
Serves 4

tip from the chef

For those who are not fond of chili ordinary baked beans can be used for this pizza instead. If you wish to make your own pizza base see the recipe for basic pizza dough and variations on page 6. Tomato dough goes great for this pizza.

three-cheese
pizza

■□□ | Cooking time: 25 minutes - Preparation time: 5 minutes

method

1. Remove about one-quarter of the dough and set aside. Press remaining dough into a lightly greased 26 x 32 cm/ 10¹/₂ x 12³/₄ in Swiss roll tin and brush with oil.

2. Roll reserved dough into two sausage shapes (a) each 26 cm/10¹/₂ in long. Place these across the pizza base (b) to divide it into three equal portions.

3. Top one-third of the pizza with blue cheese and pine nuts, another third with mozzarella cheese and oregano leaves and remaining third with Parmesan cheese and black pepper to taste (c).

4. Bake at 200°C/400°F/Gas 6 for 20-25 minutes or until cheese is golden and base is crisp.

ingredients

> **1 quantity basic pizza dough (page 6)**
> **2 teaspoons vegetable oil**
> **200 g/6¹/₂ oz blue cheese, crumbled**
> **60 g/2 oz pine nuts**
> **125 g/4 oz mozzarella cheese, grated**
> **2 tablespoons fresh oregano leaves or ¹/₂ teaspoon dried oregano**
> **90 g/3 oz Parmesan cheese, grated**
> **freshly ground black pepper**

....
Serves 4

tip from the chef

Serve this deliciously rich cheese pizza with a salad of raw or steamed mixed vegetables tossed in a light French or Italian dressing.

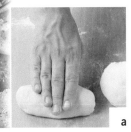

a

b

c

garden pizza

■□□ | Cooking time: 25 minutes - Preparation time: 10 minutes

ingredients

> 1 quantity basic pizza dough (page 6)
> 250 g/8 oz asparagus spears, cut into 4 cm/ 1¹/2 in pieces
> 125 g/4 oz baby yellow zucchini, sliced
> 3 spring onions, chopped
> 155 g/5 oz broccoli, cut into flowerets
> 125 g/4 oz small peas
> 2 tablespoons chopped fresh basil or 1 teaspoon dried basil
> 60 g/2 oz grated mozzarella cheese
> 60 g/2 oz grated Parmesan cheese
> freshly ground black pepper

method

1. Shape dough into a 30 cm/12 in round and place on a lightly greased baking tray.
2. Arrange asparagus, zucchini, spring onions, broccoli, peas and basil over dough. Sprinkle with mozzarella cheese, Parmesan cheese and black pepper to taste.
3. Bake at 200°C/400°F/Gas 6 for 20-25 minutes or until cheese is golden and base is crisp.

....
Serves 4

tip from the chef

Remember that pizzas do not have to be large and round. Some are rectangles, some oval, some small individual circles and some have a deep crust and sides more resembling a pie. So make your pizzas whatever shape you like.

deep-dish
pizza

■□□ | Cooking time: 30 minutes - Preparation time: 10 minutes

method

1. Press dough into the base and up the sides of a lightly greased 23 cm/9 in springform tin to form a 4 cm/1 1/2 in rim. Spread dough with tomato paste (purée).

2. Heat oil in a frying pan over a medium heat. Add garlic and spinach and cook, stirring, for 3 minutes or until spinach wilts. Drain spinach mixture well and spread over dough.

3. Top spinach with mushrooms, red pepper and oregano, then sprinkle with Parmesan cheese and season to taste with black pepper.

4. Bake at 200°C/400°F/Gas 6 for 25 minutes or until cheese is golden and base is crisp.

....
Serves 4

ingredients

> **1 quantity basic pizza dough (page 6)**
> **4 tablespoons tomato paste (purée)**
> **2 teaspoons olive oil**
> **2 cloves garlic, crushed**
> **8 leaves spinach, shredded**
> **125 g/4 oz mixed mushrooms**
> **1 red pepper, chopped**
> **2 tablespoons chopped fresh oregano or 1 teaspoon dried oregano**
> **60 g/2 oz Parmesan cheese, grated**
> **freshly ground black pepper**

tip from the chef

Fresh Parmesan cheese is available from delicatessens and some supermarkets. It is best purchased in a piece then grated as required. Once you have tried fresh Parmesan you will realize that it has a much milder and better flavor than the grated powder that comes in packets.

pizza slice

■□□ | Cooking time: 35 minutes - Preparation time: 10 minutes

ingredients

> 1 quantity wholemeal pizza dough (page 6)
> 1 tablespoon oil
> 1 onion, chopped
> 400 g/14 oz canned tomatoes, undrained
> 1/2 teaspoon dried oregano
> 1/2 teaspoon dried basil
> 1/4 cup tomato paste (purée)
> 1/2 cup sliced mushrooms
> 2 spring onions, chopped
> 125 g/4 oz ham, chopped
> 1 tablespoon black olives
> 1 cup grated mozzarella cheese

method

1. Roll out dough to line a 28 x 35 cm/ 11 x 14 in baking tray.
2. Heat oil in a frying pan, cook onion for 5 minutes, add tomatoes, oregano and basil. Crush tomatoes with spoon (a). Reduce heat, simmer for 10 minutes, cool.
3. Spread tomato paste over dough, then spread with onion mixture (b). Sprinkle evenly with mushrooms, spring onions, ham and olives, then mozzarella cheese (c).
4. Bake in moderately hot oven for 20 minutes or until golden. Cut into 12 squares.

....

Serves 6

tip from the chef

Leftover pizza is delicious in packed lunches or can be frozen.

a

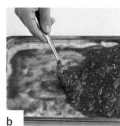

b

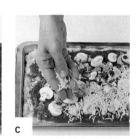

c

flatbread
pizza

■☐☐ | Cooking time: 20 minutes - Preparation time: 5 minutes

method

1. Spread tomato paste over each flatbread round.
2. Sprinkle ham, cheese and parsley on top.
3. Bake in moderate oven for 15-20 minutes.

Each round makes 6 slices

ingredients

> **2 flatbread rounds**
> **2 tablespoons tomato paste**
> **1 cup chopped ham**
> **1 cup grated Cheddar cheese**
> **1 tablespoon chopped parsley**

tip from the chef

When you're in a hurry, another option for a quick pizza base can be prepared with four sheets of filo pastry layered together with melted margarine or oil.

prosciutto
and fig pizzas

■□□ | Cooking time: 15 minutes - Preparation time: 10 minutes

ingredients

- > **1 quantity basic pizza dough (page 6)**
- > **2 teaspoons olive oil**
- > **125 g/4 oz prosciutto**
- > **4 fresh or dried figs, sliced**
- > **60 g/2 oz pine nuts**
- > **1 tablespoon chopped fresh rosemary or 1/2 teaspoon dried rosemary**
- > **freshly ground black pepper**

method

1. Divide dough into four portions and shape each to form a 15 cm/6 in round. Place rounds on lightly greased baking trays.
2. Brush dough with oil and top with prosciutto and fig slices. Sprinkle with pine nuts, rosemary and black pepper to taste.
3. Bake at 190°C/375°F/Gas 5 for 15 minutes or until bases are crisp and golden.

....

Serves 4

tip from the chef

Perfect for an autumn luncheon when fresh figs are in season and at their best.
For a complete meal accompany with garlic bread, a salad and a glass of dry white wine.

pancetta
and pear pizzas

■□□ | Cooking time: 20 minutes - Preparation time: 5 minutes

method

1. Divide dough into four portions and shape each to form a 15 cm/6 in round. Place rounds on lightly greased baking trays.
2. Cover dough with pancetta or ham. Arrange pear slices attractively on top, then sprinkle with cheese and walnuts.
3. Bake at 200°C/400°F/Gas 6 for 15-20 minutes or until base is crisp and golden.
4. Just prior to serving, toss rocket with vinegar and pile on top of pizzas. Season to taste with black pepper and serve immediately.

....

Serves 4

ingredients

> 1 quantity basic pizza dough (page 6)
> 155 g/5 oz pancetta or ham, thinly sliced
> 2 firm pears, cored, peeled and sliced
> 100 g/3$^{1}/_{2}$ oz creamy blue cheese, such as Gorgonzola, crumbled
> 60 g/2 oz walnuts, chopped
> 125 g/4 oz rocket, roughly chopped
> 2 tablespoons balsamic or red wine vinegar
> freshly ground black pepper

tip from the chef

A pizza dough made with olive oil has a crisp exterior and a tender center. Many professional pizza-makers will also brush the dough with olive oil before topping –this prevents it from drying out and helps ensure a golden color.

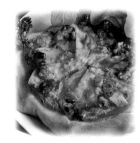

pizza
suprema

■□□ I Cooking time: 30 minutes - Preparation time: 10 minutes

ingredients

- > **2 quantities basic pizza dough (page 6)**
- > **3/4 cup/185 ml/6 fl oz tomato paste (purée)**
- > **1 green pepper, chopped**
- > **155 g/5 oz peperoni or salami, sliced**
- > **155 g/5 oz ham or prosciutto, sliced**
- > **125 g/4 oz mushrooms, sliced**
- > **440 g/14 oz canned pineapple pieces, drained**
- > **60 g/2 oz pitted olives**
- > **125 g/4 oz mozzarella cheese, grated**
- > **125 g/4 oz tasty cheese (mature Cheddar), grated**

method

1. Divide dough into two portions and shape each to form a 30 cm/12 in round. Place rounds on lightly greased baking trays.
2. Spread dough with tomato paste (purée). Arrange half the green pepper, peperoni or salami, ham or prosciutto, mushrooms, pineapple and olives attractively on each pizza base.
3. Combine mozzarella cheese and tasty cheese (mature Cheddar) and sprinkle half the mixture over each pizza.
4. Bake at 200°C/400°F/Gas 6 for 25-30 minutes or until cheese is golden and base is crisp.

....

Serves 8

tip from the chef

You might want to make only one pizza, but remember everyone loves pizza and they always eat more than you –or they– think they will.

pizza
muffins

■□□ | Cooking time: 5 minutes - Preparation time: 5 minutes

method

1. Butter each muffin half. Toast under grill until golden.
2. Spread with tomato purée and top with carrot, celery, ham and mozzarella cheese.
3. Place under hot grill until cheese melts. Serve immediately.

....
Makes 2

ingredients

> 1 wholegrain muffin, cut in half
> butter
> 1 tablespoon tomato purée
> 1/2 carrot, grated
> 1/2 stick celery, finely chopped
> 1 slice ham, chopped
> 1/2 cup mozzarella cheese

tip from the chef

Ideal for hungry ones to fill them up until dinner time.

peperoni
pizzas

■□□ | Cooking time: 30 minutes - Preparation time: 10 minutes

method

1. Shape dough into two 30 cm/12 in rounds and place on lightly greased baking trays.
2. Spread dough with tomato paste (purée), then top each base with half the peperoni and cabanossi. Arrange half the mushrooms and green pepper on each pizza and sprinkle each with half the mozzarella cheese.
3. Bake at 200°C/400°F/Gas 6 for 25-30 minutes or until cheese is golden and base is crisp.

....
Serves 10

ingredients

- > **2 quantities basic pizza dough (page 6)**
- > **³/₄ cup/185 ml/6 fl oz tomato paste (purée)**
- > **20 slices peperoni**
- > **20 slices cabanossi**
- > **200 g/6¹/₂ oz button mushrooms, sliced**
- > **1 green pepper, chopped**
- > **250 g/8 oz mozzarella cheese, grated**

tip from the chef

A pizza party can be a great way to entertain a group of young people and to get them involved with cooking. As the dough needs some time to rise it is a good idea to prepare it in advance (or use purchased pizza bases). At the time of the party lay out the ingredients for topping the pizzas and allow the guests to shape and top their own pizzas –you may be surprised at some of the combinations.

pesto pizzettas

■□□ | Cooking time: 10 minutes - Preparation time: 5 minutes

ingredients

> **4 small pitta bread rounds**
> **1/2 cup/125 g/4 oz ready-made pesto**
> **12 slices spicy salami**
> **12 cherry tomatoes, halved**
> **60 g/2 oz Parmesan cheese, grated**

method

1. Spread pitta bread rounds with pesto. Top with salami and tomatoes and sprinkle with Parmesan cheese.
2. Place bread rounds on a baking tray and bake at 200°C/400°F/Gas 6 for 10 minutes or until cheese melts and bread is crisp.

....
Serves 4

tip from the chef

Serve with a salad of mixed greens, black olives, avocado slices and chopped tomatoes tossed with an Italian dressing.

mini
pizza triangles

■☐☐ | Cooking time: 20 minutes - Preparation time: 10 minutes

method

1. Spread each pitta bread round with tomato pasta sauce, then top with green pepper and onion (a).
2. Top two pitta bread rounds with prawns and pineapple. Top the remaining two with salami and mushrooms (b). Sprinkle pizzas with cheese (c).
3. Bake at 180°C/350°F/Gas 4 for 20 minutes or until cheese is melted and bread is crisp. Cut into triangles and serve.

....
Serves 8

ingredients

> **4 pitta bread rounds**
> **1 cup/250 ml/8 fl oz tomato pasta sauce**
> **1 green pepper, chopped**
> **1 red onion, chopped**
> **220 g/7 oz small prawns, peeled, or 125 g/4 oz canned prawns, drained**
> **3 tablespoons chopped pineapple pieces**
> **125 g/4 oz salami, chopped**
> **100 g/3½ oz button mushrooms, sliced**
> **125 g/4 oz mozzarella cheese, grated**

tip from the chef

Children will love these crisp pizza triangles. Serve them hot as an after-school snack, warm at birthday parties or cold in packed lunches. And remember that, of course, toppings can be changed to suit individual tastes.

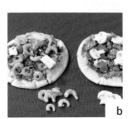

a   b   c

smoked
salmon pizzas

■ □ □ | Cooking time: 25 minutes - Preparation time: 10 minutes

method

1. Divide dough into four portions and shape each to form a 15 cm/6 in round. Place rounds on lightly greased baking trays, brush with oil and bake at 200°C/400°F/Gas 6 for 15 minutes or until crisp and golden.

2. Reduce oven temperature to 180°C/350°F/Gas 4. Top pizzas with smoked salmon and black pepper to taste and bake for 8 minutes or until salmon is hot.

3. Just prior to serving, top pizzas with crème fraîche or sour cream and caviar (if using) and sprinkle with thyme.

....
Serves 4

ingredients

- > **1 quantity basic pizza dough (page 6)**
- > **1 tablespoon olive oil**
- > **200 g/6^1/2 oz smoked salmon slices**
- > **freshly ground black pepper**
- > **4 tablespoons crème fraîche or sour cream**
- > **4 teaspoons caviar (optional)**
- > **2 tablespoons chopped fresh lemon thyme**

tip from the chef

If lemon thyme is unavailable you can use ^{1}/2 teaspoon dried thyme and ^{1}/2 teaspoon finely grated lemon rind. Sprinkle thyme over pizza bases at the beginning of cooking and sprinkle lemon rind over pizzas just prior to serving.

french
pissaladière

■□□ | Cooking time: 55 minutes - Preparation time: 10 minutes

method

1. Divide dough into two portions and press each into a lightly greased 26 x 32 cm/ 10½ x 12¾ in Swiss roll tin.
2. To make topping, heat oil in a saucepan over a medium heat. Add onions and garlic and cook, stirring, for 10 minutes or until onions are soft. Reduce heat to low, add thyme and sugar and cook, stirring frequently, for 20 minutes or until mixture is thick and caramelized.
3. Spread half the onion mixture over each pizza base, then top with anchovy fillets, olives, capers, pine nuts and black pepper to taste.
4. Bake at 200°C/400°F/Gas 6 for 20-25 minutes or until base is crisp and golden.

....
Serves 8

ingredients

- > **2 quantities basic pizza dough (page 6)**
- > **24 anchovy fillets**
- > **125 g/4 oz pitted black olives**
- > **2 tablespoons capers, drained**
- > **60 g/2 oz pine nuts**
- > **freshly ground black pepper**

onion topping

- > **2 tablespoons olive oil**
- > **8 onions, thinly sliced**
- > **6 cloves garlic, crushed**
- > **2 tablespoons chopped fresh thyme or 1 teaspoon dried thyme**
- > **2 tablespoons sugar**

tip from the chef

Originating from the Provence region of France this delicious onion, anchovy and olive topped bread is the French equivalent of the Italian pizza.

salmon
and avocado pizza

■□□ | Cooking time: 25 minutes - Preparation time: 10 minutes

method

1. Press dough into a greased 26 x 32 cm/ 10½ x 12¾ in Swiss roll tin.
2. Place ricotta cheese, dill and thyme in a bowl and mix to combine. Spread mixture over pizza base and bake at 200°C/400°F/Gas 6 for 15 minutes.
3. Top pizza with smoked salmon, avocado slices, capers and tomatoes. Reduce oven temperature to 180°C/350°F/Gas 4 and bake for 10 minutes longer or until heated through and base is crisp and golden.

....
Serves 4

ingredients

> **1 quantity basic pizza dough (page 6)**
> **200 g/6½ oz ricotta cheese, drained**
> **2 tablespoons chopped fresh dill**
> **1 tablespoon chopped fresh lemon thyme or ½ teaspoon dried thyme and 1 teaspoon finely grated lemon rind**
> **250 g/8 oz smoked salmon slices**
> **1 avocado, stoned, peeled and sliced**
> **1 tablespoon capers, drained**
> **125 g/4 oz cherry tomatoes, halved**

tip from the chef

Other easy pizza bases include purchased focaccia bread, pitta bread rounds, hamburger buns and muffins. You will need to adjust the cooking time of your pizza, as different bases may affect it.

sardine
and lime pizza

■□□ | Cooking time: 30 minutes - Preparation time: 10 minutes

ingredients
- > **1 quantity basic pizza dough (page 6)**
- > **2 teaspoons olive oil**
- > **3 red onions, sliced**
- > **3 cloves garlic, crushed**
- > **3 tablespoons chopped fresh mixed herbs**
- > **200 g/7 oz canned sardines, drained**
- > **1 tablespoon finely grated lime rind**
- > **1 tablespoon lime juice**
- > **freshly ground black pepper**

method
1. Shape dough to form a 1 cm/½ in thick round with a 30 cm/12 in diameter. Place on a lightly greased baking tray (a).
2. Heat oil in a frying pan over a low heat. Add onions and garlic and cook, stirring, for 5 minutes or until onions are soft. Add herbs (b) and mix to combine.
3. Spread onion mixture over pizza base, top with sardines (c), sprinkle with lime rind, lime juice and black pepper to taste.
4. Bake at 220°C/425°F/Gas 7 for 10 minutes, then reduce oven temperature to 190°C/375°F/Gas 5 and bake for 15 minutes longer or until base is crisp and golden.

Serves 4

tip from the chef
Use whatever herbs are in season for this pizza. For a traditional combination dill and parsley are delicious or for a Thai feel why not try coriander, basil and parsley.

a

b

c

chili
prawn pizza

■□□ | Cooking time: 25 minutes - Preparation time: 10 minutes

method

1. Shape dough to form a 30 cm/12 in round. Place on a lightly greased baking tray, spread with tomato paste (purée).
2. Heat oil in a frying pan over a medium heat, add cumin, chilies and garlic and cook, stirring, for 1 minute. Stir in lemon juice and prawns and cook for 3 minutes longer or until prawns just change color and are almost cooked.
3. Top pizza base with red pepper, yellow or green pepper, then with prawn mixture, coriander, Parmesan cheese and black pepper to taste.
4. Bake at 200°C/400°F/Gas 6 for 20 minutes or until base is crisp and golden.

....
Serves 4

ingredients

> **1 quantity basic pizza dough (page 6)**
> **3 tablespoons tomato paste (purée)**
> **2 teaspoons vegetable oil**
> **1 teaspoon ground cumin**
> **3 fresh red chilies, seeded and chopped**
> **2 cloves garlic, crushed**
> **2 tablespoons lemon juice**
> **500 g/1 lb uncooked prawns, shelled and deveined**
> **1 red pepper, sliced**
> **1 yellow or green pepper, sliced**
> **2 tablespoons chopped fresh coriander**
> **2 tablespoons grated Parmesan cheese**
> **freshly ground black pepper**

tip from the chef

For a complete meal accompany this tasty pizza with a salad of mixed lettuces and fresh herbs.

satay
chicken pizzas

■□□ I Cooking time: 25 minutes - Preparation time: 10 minutes

ingredients

- > **2 quantities basic pizza dough (page 6)**
- > **1 cup/250 ml/8 fl oz satay sauce**
- > **1 red pepper, sliced**
- > **1 green pepper, sliced**
- > **1 carrot, cut into thin strips**
- > **100 g/3½ oz bean sprouts**
- > **1 cooked chicken, flesh cut into small pieces**
- > **185 g/6 oz tasty cheese (mature Cheddar), grated**

method

1. Shape dough into two 30 cm/12 in rounds and place on lightly greased baking trays.
2. Spread dough with satay sauce. Arrange half the red pepper, green pepper, carrot and bean sprouts on each pizza base. Top each base with half the chicken and sprinkle each with half the cheese.
3. Bake at 200°C/400°F/Gas 6 for 20-25 minutes or until cheese is golden and base is crisp.

....
Serves 10

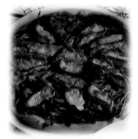

tip from the chef

This pizza is also delicious made with cold roast beef, lamb or turkey.

oriental
chicken pizza

■ □ □ | Cooking time: 30 minutes - Preparation time: 5 minutes

method

1. Place pizza base on a lightly greased baking tray.
2. Spread base with teriyaki sauce and top with chicken, snow peas, spring onions, tofu and asparagus. Sprinkle with coriander and sesame seeds. Drizzle chili sauce over pizza.
3. Bake at 200°C/400°F/Gas 6 for 30 minutes or until base is golden and crisp.

....
Serves 4

ingredients

> **1 x 30 cm/12 in pizza base, homemade or purchased**
> **1/4 cup/60 ml/2 fl oz thick teriyaki sauce**
> **2 boneless chicken breast fillets, cooked and sliced**
> **125 g/4 oz snow peas, thinly sliced**
> **4 spring onions, sliced**
> **155 g/5 oz tofu, chopped**
> **6 asparagus spears, cut into 5 cm/2 in pieces**
> **3 tablespoons chopped fresh coriander**
> **3 tablespoons sesame seeds, toasted**
> **2 tablespoons sweet chili sauce**

tip from the chef
Sweet soy sauce known as kechap manis can be used instead of teriyaki in this recipe if you wish.

mushroom
chicken pizzas

■□□ I Cooking time: 20 minutes - Preparation time: 5 minutes

ingredients

> 4 x 15 cm/6 in squares focaccia bread
> 1/2 cup/125 ml/4 fl oz tomato pasta sauce
> 90 g/3 oz chopped cooked chicken
> 8 mushrooms, chopped
> 1 green pepper, chopped
> 4 spring onions, finely chopped
> 4 pitted black olives, sliced
> 60 g/2 oz Cheddar cheese, grated
> 30 g/1 oz grated Parmesan cheese

method

1. Spread each square of focaccia with tomato sauce. Top with chicken, mushrooms, green pepper, spring onions and olives. Combine Cheddar and Parmesan cheeses and sprinkle over chicken and vegetables.
2. Place pizzas on nonstick baking trays and bake at 180°C/350°F/Gas 4 for 20 minutes or until cheese is melted and golden brown.

....
Serves 4

tip from the chef

These pizzas are just as delicious cold as hot, so make extras and have them for lunch the next day.

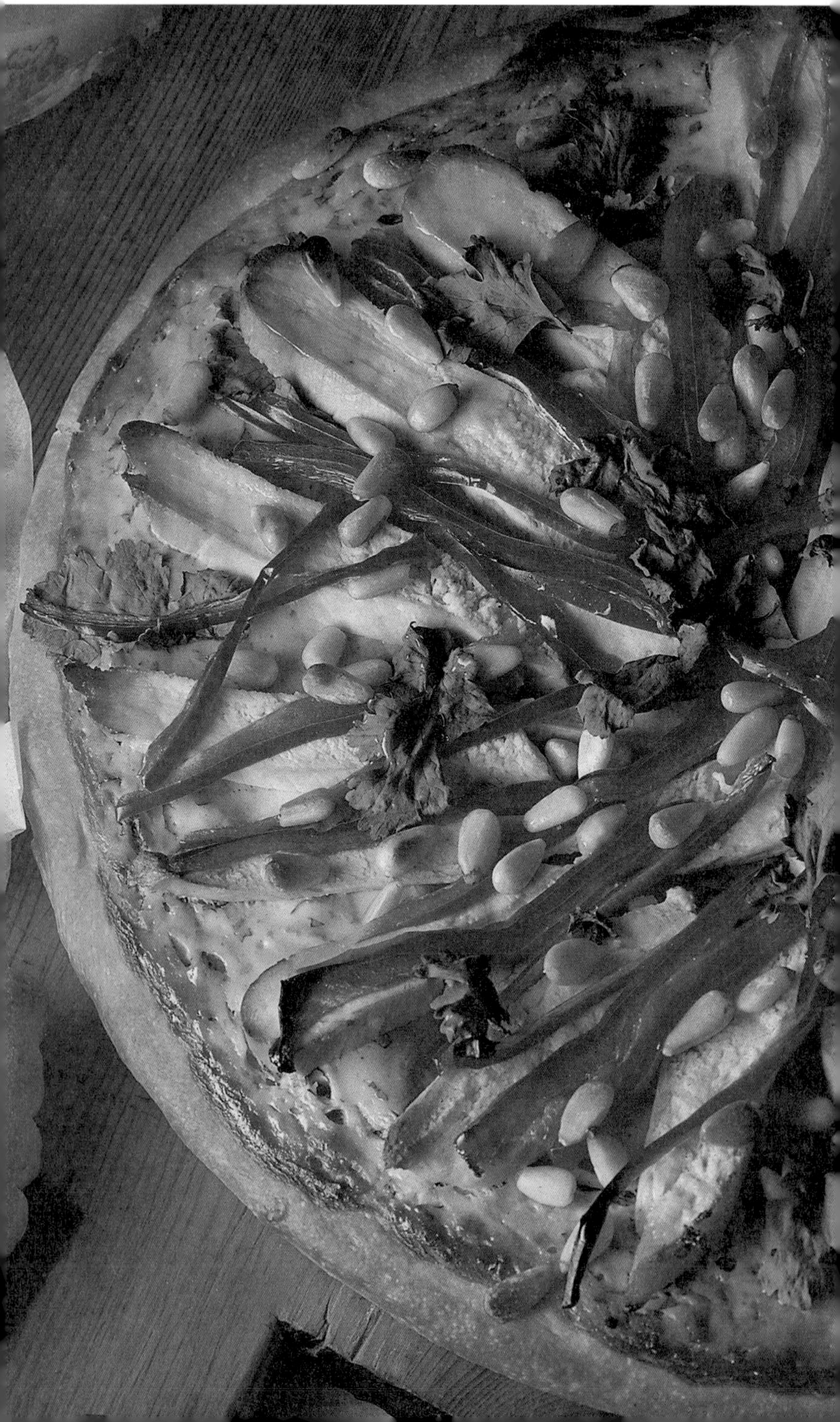

yogurt chicken pizza

■□□ | Cooking time: 30 minutes - Preparation time: 10 minutes

method

1. Shape dough to form a 30 cm/12 in round. Place on a lightly greased baking tray.
2. Place yogurt, mint and chutney in a bowl and mix to combine. Spread yogurt mixture over pizza base and bake at 200°C/400°F/Gas 6 for 15 minutes.
3. Top pizza with chicken, red pepper, coriander leaves and pine nuts and bake for 10-15 minutes longer or until topping is heated through and base is crisp and golden.

Serves 4

ingredients

> **1 quantity basic pizza dough (page 6)**
> **1/2 cup/100 g/3 1/2 oz natural yogurt**
> **1 tablespoon chopped fresh mint**
> **1 tablespoon mango chutney**
> **250 g/8 oz cooked chicken, chopped**
> **1 red pepper, thinly sliced**
> **1 tablespoon fresh coriander leaves**
> **3 tablespoons pine nuts**

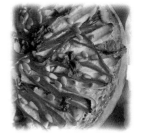

tip from the chef
A great way to turn leftover cooked chicken into something special.

thai
beef pizzas

■□□ | Cooking time: 30 minutes - Preparation time: 15 minutes

method

1. To make marinade, place garlic, soy sauce, lemon grass and coriander in a large bowl and mix to combine.
2. Heat a nonstick frying pan over a high heat, add steak and cook for 1 minute each side. Remove steak from pan and slice thinly. Add steak to marinade, cover and set aside to marinate for 15 minutes.
3. Shape dough into two 30 cm/12 in rounds or two 15 x 25 cm/6 x 10 in rectangles and place on lightly greased baking trays.
4. Combine tomato purée and chili sauce, spread over pizza bases and bake at 200°C/400°F/Gas 6 for 15 minutes.
5. Top pizza bases with spring onions, carrot and celery, then arrange beef slices attractively on top and bake for 10 minutes longer or until topping is heated through and base is crisp and golden.

Serves 8

ingredients

> 500 g/1 lb rump steak, trimmed of all visible fat
> 2 quantities basic pizza dough (page 6)
> 3 tablespoons tomato purée
> 2 tablespoons sweet chili sauce
> 3 spring onions, chopped
> 1 carrot, cut into matchsticks
> 2 stalks celery, cut into matchsticks

thai marinade

> 1 clove garlic, crushed
> 3 tablespoons soy sauce
> 1 stalk fresh lemon grass, chopped, or 1 teaspoon dried lemon grass or 1 teaspoon finely grated lemon rind
> 3 tablespoons chopped fresh coriander

tip from the chef
Combining two popular cuisines, this pizza is ideal to serve when you can't decide whether to choose Oriental or Mediterranean.

pesto
vegetable calzone

■ ■ □ | Cooking time: 30 minutes - Preparation time: 10 minutes

ingredients

> **2 quantities basic pizza dough (page 6)**
> **olive oil**

pesto vegetable filling

> **2 eggplant, sliced**
> **vegetable oil**
> **1 red pepper, chopped**
> **1 green pepper, chopped**
> **2 zucchini, chopped**
> **3/4 cup/185 g/6 oz ready-made pesto**
> **4 bocconcini or 125 g/4 oz mozzarella cheese, chopped**
> **3 tablespoons pine nuts**
> **freshly ground black pepper**

method

1. To make filling, brush eggplant slices with a little oil and cook under a preheated hot grill for 3-4 minutes each side or until golden. Drain on absorbent kitchen paper and chop.
2. Heat 1 tablespoon oil in a frying pan over a medium heat, add red pepper, green pepper, zucchini and pesto and cook, stirring, for 3 minutes or until vegetables are soft. Mix in eggplant and set aside to cool. Add cheese, pine nuts and black pepper to taste to vegetable mixture and mix to combine.
3. Divide dough into 8 portions and shape each to form a 5 mm/1/4 in thick round with a 15 cm/6 in diameter.
4. Place spoonfuls of filling in the center of each dough round, brush the edges with water, then fold over to form a half circle. Press edges together to seal and using a fork make a decorative pattern.
5. Brush calzone with oil, place on lightly greased baking trays and bake at 200°C/400°F/Gas 6 for 20 minutes or until puffed and golden.

....
Makes 8

tip from the chef

Calzone is basically a pizza folded over to encase the filling. These individual calzoni make great finger food for an informal party and leftovers are a welcome addition to a packed lunch.

four-cheese
calzone

■ ■ □ | Cooking time: 15 minutes - Preparation time: 10 minutes

method

1. To make filling, place ricotta cheese, tasty cheese (mature Cheddar), Swiss cheese, mozzarella cheese, chives and black pepper to taste in a bowl and mix to combine.
2. Divide dough into 10 portions. Shape each portion into a 5 mm/1/4 in thick round with a 15 cm/6 in diameter.
3. Place spoonfuls of filling in the center of each round, brush edges with water, then fold over to form a half circle. Press edges together to seal.
4. Brush calzone with olive oil, place on lightly greased baking trays and bake at 200°C/400°F/Gas 6 for 15 minutes or until puffed and golden.

....
Makes 10

ingredients

- > **2 quantities basic pizza dough (page 6)**
- > **olive oil**

cheese filling

- > **200 g/6 1/2 oz ricotta cheese, drained**
- > **60 g/2 oz tasty cheese (mature Cheddar), grated**
- > **60 g/2 oz Swiss cheese, grated**
- > **60 g/2 oz mozzarella cheese, grated**
- > **3 tablespoons snipped fresh chives**
- > **freshly ground pepper**

tip from the chef

These crisp parcels contain a rich smooth cheese filling. Blue cheese lovers will enjoy calzone made with blue cheese in place of the Swiss cheese.

prosciutto
and cheese calzone

■ ■ □ | Cooking time: 20 minutes - Preparation time: 10 minutes

ingredients

> **2 quantities basic pizza dough (page 6)**
> **olive oil**

prosciutto and cheese filling

> **200 g/6¹/2 oz ricotta cheese, drained**
> **14 slices prosciutto or lean ham, chopped**
> **125 g/4 oz Provolone or Parmesan cheese, grated**
> **30 g/1 oz sun-dried tomatoes, chopped**
> **60 g/2 oz pitted black olives, chopped**
> **2 tablespoons chopped fresh basil**

method

1. To make filling, place ricotta cheese, prosciutto or ham, Provolone or Parmesan cheese, sun-dried tomatoes, olives and basil in a bowl and mix to combine.
2. Divide dough into 8 portions and shape each to form a 5 mm/¹/4 in thick round with a 15 cm/6 in diameter.
3. Place spoonfuls of filling in the center of each dough round (a), brush the edges with water, then fold over to form a half circle. Press edges together to seal (b) and using a fork make a decorative pattern.
4. Brush calzone with oil (c), place on lightly greased baking trays and bake at 200°C/400°F/Gas 6 for 20 minutes or until puffed and golden.

....
Makes 8

tip from the chef

A salad of mixed lettuces tossed with balsamic vinegar makes a wonderful accompaniment to calzone.

a

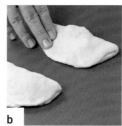

b

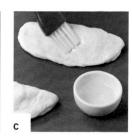

c

index